Pink and Prey...

Unveiling the Depths of Women's
Resilience and Suffering

Sumedha Bhaduri

BookLeaf Publishing

India | USA | UK

Copyright @ Sumedha Bhaduri
All Rights Reserved.

This book has been self-published with all reasonable efforts taken to make the material error-free by the author. No part of this book shall be used, reproduced in any manner whatsoever without written permission from the author, except in the case of brief quotations embodied in critical articles and reviews.

The Author of this book is solely responsible and liable for its content including but not limited to the views, representations, descriptions, statements, information, opinions, and references ["Content"]. The Content of this book shall not constitute or be construed or deemed to reflect the opinion or expression of the Publisher or Editor. Neither the Publisher nor Editor endorse or approve the Content of this book or guarantee the reliability, accuracy, or completeness of the Content published herein and do not make any representations or warranties of any kind, express or implied, including but not limited to the implied warranties of merchantability, fitness for a particular purpose.

The Publisher and Editor shall not be liable whatsoever...

Made with ❤ on the BookLeaf Publishing Platform
www.bookleafpub.in
www.bookleafpub.com

Dedication

To all the women of the world, in all your diverse and beautiful forms—

This book is a tribute to your resilience, your love, your pain, and your joy.

To the mothers who give endlessly, the daughters who strive, the sisters who support, and the children who inspire. To the women in every profession, in every walk of life—may these words honor the voices you carry and bring light to the stories that deserve to be heard.

Acknowledgement

I would like to extend my heartfelt gratitude to all the incredible women who inspire me everyday. To those who brighten our lives and those who fight silent battles with strength and grace—this book is a tribute to you. Your courage and resilience are the heartbeat of these poems.

A special thank you to my family and friends for their unwavering support and encouragement throughout this journey. I am profoundly grateful to my sister for her trust, support, and the special role she has played in my life. Your presence and faith in me have been a constant source of inspiration.

To my readers, thank you for opening your hearts to my words. Your willingness to engage with and share these poems is a gift beyond measure. I hope they bring you as much meaning and connection as they brought to me while writing them.

Last, but certainly not least, I give my deepest thanks to God for guiding me through this journey and for the countless blessings that have made this book a reality.

Preface

In the quiet spaces between words and the soft hum of emotions lies the essence of what it means to be a woman. This collection of poems, *Pink and Prey...*, is a journey into those quiet spaces—a poetic exploration of the diverse and profound experiences of women.

Throughout history, women have navigated a complex tapestry of emotions and experiences. From the tender moments of love and the deep bonds of friendship to the harsh realities of struggle and resilience, this book aims to capture the multifaceted nature of womanhood. Each poem sheds light on the joys, sorrows, and unspoken battles that define our lives.

The poems in this collection span various genres, each capturing different aspects of emotions and struggles. The order in which the poems are presented is intentionally

unstructured, mirroring the reality that women's experiences are not linear but rather a rollercoaster of emotions. A woman may be vulnerable today, yet an ultimate
source of power tomorrow; she might be sad one day but, the next, mask her pain with a smile and heal others' souls. This book seeks to encapsulate the spectrum of her emotions, sometimes even within the span of a single day.

As I wrote these verses, I found myself immersed in the stories of women who make life more vibrant, fight silent battles with courage, and persist with unyielding strength. This book is dedicated to them—the unsung heroines who inspire with their everyday acts of bravery and love.

As you turn the pages, I invite you to delve into the world of *Pink and Prey...* with an open heart and a receptive mind. May these poems speak to the depths of your own experiences, and may they offer a voice to the silent echoes within.

Towards A Calm Abyss

Let the stars shine before I sleep.
Let the moon smile in the night deep.
Let tranquility end all the chaos,
Let me know if you see the odds.

Adoring the airglow in the sky,
I forget that some moments are a lie.
Closing my eyes for a false dream,
Hoping it brings me happiness, serene.

Tired of keeping the lies alive,
My heart ponders in a deep dive,
Capturing those fireflies in the dark night,
To give this life a spark of light.

Trying to escape an enigmatic wood,
I discover truths misunderstood.
Realizing healing is the ultimate bliss,
I am moving towards a calm abyss.

In Love's Embrace

It's just that when I look at the moon,
I feel like losing myself to nature's favorite
tune.
The wind around me sets my soul free,
I feel like you are so close to me.

Through the stills of life captured in our
mural,
Your stars shine the brightest, even in colors
simple.
Please don't leave me ever,
For this is meant to be forever.

You saw me at my worst and still never left
me alone,
I never knew that loving someone so deeply
could feel like home.
Hold on to me, even if the darkness in me
unwinds my soul,
I promise to be worthy of your love and never
leave you alone.

Even when the night falls, I will be there with
you.
Let me live in you for this moment, and
forever true.
In love's embrace, we find our endless rhyme,
Two hearts entwined, forever through all
time.

Hope

Don't be so strong that you break me.
Don't be so sweet that you melt me.
Don't care for me if you would leave me.
Don't destroy me if you love me.
Don't promise me if you would lie to me.
Don't question me if you said you would trust
me.

Don't let me lose myself.
Don't let me kill myself.
Just help me know my worth and find my
way,

To reach a place where peace stays.
It may be for today or forever,
But don't make me a melted candle if you
don't hate me.

Since...

Smiles scarred and a broken heart
Wish to move toward a new start.
Drenched in pain, with hope to heal,
Choosing a path that guides to peace.
This little heart, burdened with illusions,
This little heart, filled with fake sweet
memories,
Wishes to move on, wishes to heal.
So, it may be for today or forever,
But don't make me a melted candle if you
don't hate me.

Realization

And just when all was at peace,
I realized something was still empty in that
heart's piece.
I tried to fill that emptiness with love,
But all I did was give it a shove.

And just when all appeared simple,
I realized complications arose from my
impulse.
I tried to calm my impulse with
understanding,
But I found myself drained from standing.

And just when all seemed so beautiful,
I realized it was a maze, pitiful.
I tried to destroy this lie and replace it with
faith,
But I grew exhausted in the wait.

Now I want to be free,
But I know it's not easy.
True freedom comes when we start loving
ourselves,
And this is only possible with the realization
of our true selves.

Assaulted To Death

Standing all alone upon a path eerie,
Every heartbeat of mine warns me of
something scary.
With each passing minute, the vicinity
darkens,
And a creepy presence begins to encircle.

Moving forward, trying to find a way out, my
fear uncontrolled,
I encounter an apparition in the night cold.
There was blood all over her.
I pleaded for it to leave, but my vision began
to blur.

I was fainting in front of the ghost;
Meanwhile, her cold hands were dragging me
to an old coast.
In the dark night, all I could hear was a voice
crying for help.
In a glimpse, the body took the form of a girl
I knew.

The girl had tears of blood in her eyes;
Weeping, she told me about her demise.
It was a night similar to this,
When she was trapped and physically
assaulted to death.

This betrayal came from someone she once
held dear.
With pain, she told me she had saved me from
this harrowing fear,
Because the same would have happened to me
in this quarter.
As the sun approached the horizon,
She warned me to trust none.
Then, in a blink, she faded away,

Leaving me to wonder: what was the real horror at the bay?

Just To Live

Face the reality
To embrace the tranquility...
Confront your fear,
To the edge that is near.
Open your heart, to yourself, just to live.

Accept what lies within,
Reveal what remains concealed,
Understand what has been forsaken,
And love, even if it's forbidden.
Open your heart, to yourself, just to live.

Eyes that reflect depths of courage,
Lips that whisper depths of truth,
A body that radiates depths of confidence—
Let us live and love ourselves,
Bringing us the freedom to accept who we
are.
So, open your heart, to yourself, just to live.

My Best Friend

It was but yesterday, I began to love 'ME,'
And this sunrise came to my life because there
was 'SHE.'
Well, she—she is my best friend,
The one with whom I wish to remain until the
very end.

Through all these years, I've seen so many,
But never found a soul like hers in any.
She came to me as a precious gift,
And gave this dull life of mine a happy lift.

Each moment shared with her is like raindrops in
a desert,
With no pain to assert.
Well, the days with calmness to spend
Will be as beautiful as if they never went.

Just to say one thing to you:
You are my best friend, etched deeply in my
heart's view.
And whatever the pandemonium future brings in
blue,
Always remember, I'll be there for you.

Falling Out Of Love

I tried hard to come out of the abyss.
At first, everything seemed to be bliss,
But then you kept haunting me in my dreams,
And every time, I tried to run away with my will
extreme.

Do you know I used to be a keeper?
But now, I avoid being a believer.
I try to hide from everything beautiful in my life,
Because I am afraid of falling again into a deep
dive.

I might again start to lose myself,
But this time, I won't let myself melt.
Today, you are again standing in front of me,
As usual, fake, but now I am glad that I can see.

Lying has always been fun for you,
But this time, I am not falling for any trap new.
I've lost all my sweetness through your shove,
So much so that now, I am falling out of love.

The Story Is Already Written

Just as every word adds essence to a sentence,
Just as every wait corresponds to a magical
acceptance,
Just as every star completes a constellation,
Just as every second concludes to a new
fascination—
It is now time for you to understand
That every moment of yours is part of a story
planned.
The struggles may seem unjust at this hand,
The world might seem cruel at every stand,
But all these are for a beautiful future,
A future you never imagined you could capture.
We don't know where we will end in our life,
But we should at least make our hearts thrive.

If we can live every moment with happiness and
hope,
Then we can beautifully draw a future and ascend
the mountain slope.

Am I So Easy To Let Go?

In shadows cast by friendship's fading glow,
If I release your hand, will you let me go?
A haunting question lingers in the silent
plea—
Will you, too, abandon me and set me free?

A tearful echo in the quiet of goodbye,
Will you chase the fragments of a fading sigh?
Or am I just a whisper, easily erased,
Lost in the void, a friendship misplaced?

If I step away, will you come to implore,
Plead for reasons, beg me to restore?

Or, in cold silence, will you turn and depart,
Leaving behind the fragments of a shattered
heart?

As I walk away on this path unknown,
Will you watch me leave, in silence, alone?
Will you understand the reasons untold,
Or the void in the story once told?

My Euphoria

I am so much in love that I long to shout it to
the world,
In this ocean of happiness, my heart's sail
unfurled.
All my senses surrender to euphoria's tender
embrace,
My heart dances like a leaf in the gentle rain's
grace.

I don't know what happens each time our eyes
meet,
But in this newfound paradise, my heart skips
a beat.

You saved me from myself; that much is true,
You made me believe in love, and in you.

I find serenity in the gaze of your eyes,
My heart flutters, soaring like a bird in the skies.
In the presence of your love, I have discovered my truth,
A symphony of emotions, ageless and ever-youth.

I Will Be Waiting By The Moon

If I feel safe this way,
Then I hope I can survive the day.
I started lonely on a path so scary,
And I hope I find my way home safely.

Passing the hurdles that I encounter every mile,
Now I feel scared, and it kills my smile.
The night is long, but I believe I can find peace
within it,
And I can pause, sit for a while, listen to music,
and wait for sunrise.

One day the wind will change, and the sun will
shine bright,

Because there are things that I will make right.
And for you, if the path ends too soon,
Don't worry—I will be waiting by the moon.

The Stranger

On a night scary, I met a stranger in
bewilderment.
I was confused and scared at the same time;
He wished to speak with me,
But I was convinced that no one would want
to talk to me.

He was a stranger but felt too known.
That night, I forgot what it feels like to be
alone.
We chatted through the night while returning
to our homes.
He said that he wanted to know me.
Well, it was strange—very strange to me—

Because who would want to know an
ordinary girl like me?

I said,
"I am someone who sees magic in music and
love in the fall,
I find depth in the shallows and forever in a
moment small.
Why do you want to know me?
Do you see beyond the darkness in this
ordinary?
Do you see the depths yet unknown?
Should I start to believe that a stranger could
be my very own?"

Then, in a glimpse, I witnessed the sunrise,
It was enchanting as I felt myself losing to the
moment's guise.
But it lasted only a moment, as always,
And the stranger reminded me that we had
reached crossroads,
And that our ways are separate now.

He said,
"Because I too must discover who I am.

Maybe the time was nice but a mistake in its
hue,
And maybe, someday, we will meet on the
other side of the day."
Then he left without even saying goodbye,
And once again I was left alone after that
beautiful night.

When I resumed my journey, I realized once
more,
That the darkness within me frightened him,
as it does to all before.
And I also realized that I need none but the
sun
To wash away the shadows and to set me free.

Sins Of Silence

Sitting here, lost in thoughts on a cloudy day,
As shadows of fear cloud the light's display.
My heart aches with a heavy, silent prayer:
What led them to this fate, so cruel and
unfair?

I heard them claim the clothes were
improper,
But what should a 5-year-old wear to stop
such a monster?
I heard them say it was her fault for being out
so late at night,
But what is she to do when her work extends
beyond the light?

They claimed she cast a flirty look at the
innocent man,
But how could an 80-year-old with blurred
vision even glance?
They claimed her character was tainted by her
company with a man,
But why should only women be judged, while
men's character is never in the span?
Excuses and blame are easy to devise,
But embracing responsibility and the harsh
truth is where society struggles and lies.
It's oh-so-easy to fight for women's rights and
all they dare,
Especially since society loves rules that make
women seem fragile and rare.

A woman is not an object, nor a liability or
responsibility;
She deserves to walk the streets freely,
without fear or hostility.
Why pray to idols of Goddesses when women
can't be treated right?
Isn't this hypocrisy, fueled by toxic
masculinity's might?

Give Me Some Time Please

Here I am again, pondering, who am I?
When the pain from the stigma makes my
soul cry.
I try to draw courage from my past triumphs,
Yet the echoes of hurt continue to haunt my
mind.

While lying on my bed, my little heart
whispers,
"It's time to let go," and a sudden pain deep
inside flickers.
A somber voice from within softly whispers,
"Do you still believe in love through all your
shivers?"

I was known to always be kind,
A soul with genuine love and a spirit divine.
I had a smile that could brighten the darkest
night,
A touch that healed souls and made
everything right.
I wonder where my smile has faded through
time—
Is it because I took their pain and drained my
love's rhyme?
Or is it because the harsh experiences silenced
my heart's dance,
Or because my heart began to yearn for a love
it never had a chance?

To walk in a world that teaches you to need
someone as you age,
How do I tell the world that my heart's out of
love and can't be a cage?
It's not that I don't desire to start love anew,
But how do I say that I simply can't trust
anyone through?

My life till now has taught me to be THE
ONE for me,
And now the world insists I need someone to
walk beside me.
If I'm to open up to someone new and let
them complete me,
Don't you think I need time to unlearn the
past and embrace what could be?
With all these questions and confusions, my
heart feels cared,
Knowing there's little time to ponder and
embrace the new that's prepared.
My soul trembles, wondering if love is truly
meant for me,
Or if I'm destined to again drain my energy.

I hope the world will understand and give me
time to grow,
To find my way to healing and let my true self
show.
I hope the world will set its rules and
timelines aside,
And see, with love, that I'm not yet ready for
the path they've tried.

Then, if not the world—

Do you believe I'll find someone who respects
my boundaries,
And patiently waits for me until I'm ready?
Do you think that I'll be lucky to find
someone who can heal my inner child,
Restore my faith in love, and make my heart
smile?

Look What You Made Me Do

In shadows deep where whispers play,
A tale unfolds of night and day.
Betrayal's sting, a venomous seed,
Ignites the flames of a vengeful need.

Beneath the moon, the secrets weep,
The wounds you carved, now secrets keep.
A dance of shadows, a haunting plea,
A twisted fate, a bound destiny.

In every verse, a silent scream,
A shattered vow, a fractured dream.
Through echoes dark, resentment grows,
A symphony where vengeance flows.

In the silence, a verdict clear,
A reckoning, drawing near.
In the darkness, I rise with might,
I reclaim my throne, a phoenix's flight.

With every word, the echoes ring,
A phoenix rises on revenge's wing.
The tale retold, emotions through—
Look what you made me do.

All Alone Again

As constellations whispered tales of
self-doubt, a belief took root,
I believed love's embrace was something I'd
live without.
Yet fate unveiled a cosmic dance, a celestial
song,
Where someone made me their first and
proved my beliefs wrong.

They adorned me with stardust, galaxies in
their gaze,
In the cosmos of their love, I found
unparalleled grace.
No longer confined by shadows, I soared high
and free,

Held in the orbit of a heart that chose to
embrace me.

Through unspoken language, a silent
symphony,
They understood the nuances, the depths
within me.
No need for explanations or linguistic art,
They perceived the language etched within
my heart.

In the script of expectations, a plot twist
unfurled,
I believed I was the first, the sole in their
world.
But the echoes of our connection from a
distant hum,
Faded like the sunset; the day was done.

In the mirror of self-doubt, reflections are
unclear,
A question echoes: "Do I truly deserve what's
near?"
Becoming distant, a shield against the pain,

Yet even in my solitude, echoes of doubt remain.

Shouting in echoes, tears paint my plea,
Yet in return, a cold wind whispers back at me.
Feelings of unworthiness, a heavy burden to bear,
As if I'm an alien, an object too selfish to bear.

In the abyss of emotions, threads worn,
A heart once open now weathered and torn.
Accused of selfishness, a control freak they claim,
Yet beneath the surface, yearnings for love aflame.

Rudeness, a language of the heart's frustration,
A defense mechanism against love's alienation.
But deep within, the yearning remains,
To shatter the barriers and release love's chains.

Amidst the echoes of rejection's cruel song,
I seek a sanctuary where I truly belong.
In the labyrinth of pain where shadows loom,
I wonder if healing will ever again find its
room.

A Mother

We can walk an extra mile or more,
To find solace and let our hearts soar.
But no place can truly calm our heart,
Except in a mother's lap, where it all starts.

She is there, always caring for us,
She is there, always supporting us.
When she keeps her soft hands on our head,
It feels as though all our worries have fled.

She is warmth, she is grace,
She is fire, she is ice.
She is tender, she is honorable,
She is extraordinary and remarkable.

For our good, she always sets things right,
With all her love, she forgets her pain and
adjusts with all her might.
Just for our happiness, she can travel
multiverses like no other,
She definitely has the strength because she is
a mother.

Trapped

I am just a little tired and longing to be free.
I need the energy to break the cage inside of me.
Every day, I try a little to break the cage,
But every time, the people around me tend to amaze.

Every day I feel a bit weaker.
It feels like falling into a deep abyss.
I can see those fairy tales fading away;
is time, the wound is deeper anyway.

It scares me to trust anyone now.
If you wish to come into my life, my heart will no longer allow.
The scars seem to mock me every day,

And the pain is trying to steal my happiness away.

But amidst all the pain, I know one thing for sure:
I will come back stronger than before.
I will never give in to this pain and fear,
And no matter what happens, the hope in me is
meant to be forever.

A Mystical Rebirth

The moon was smiling bright at me today,
The butterflies came to take my pain away.
I can again see the clear waters,
I can again feel the mystical wonders.

Yesterday, the night was the darkest,
I felt lost in the deep forest.
My soul wanted to leave me amidst the agony,
I begged it to stay, promising ecstasy.

Now, I wish for a beautiful, mystical enigma
for tomorrow,
To bring peace to my mind—a mystery I wish
to borrow.

Believing once more in the magic of falling
stars as gifts from Asteria,
I want to surrender myself to this sublime
euphoria.

Something For You

Roses are red, violets are blue,
There is something that I want you to know.

The rainbow has colors seven,
Likewise, we have emotions that seem to be
gifts from heaven.

Well, these are just lies of those moments,
Because beware of the later torments.

Don't write your tale in the dark depth,
And blame yourself with every step.

Paint a life that you believe.
Others' lives would make it hard for you to
live.

Learn today because you get this chance;
You never know when it's your last dance.

Believe that the wind will take all your doubts
away,
And with hope, you will find peace forever to
stay.

Today you might fall again,
But promise yourself you'll rise again.

Just stay calm and take a few days of rest;
Then you'll be ready for whatever the world
has next.

The shadows might start haunting you again,
The pain might find its way again.

You might feel so empty;
I know loneliness is so scary.

Amidst the ocean of expectations,
Here you stand, wondering at the edges of
limitations.

With the desire to find who is hiding within
yourself,
You must ask a question to set yourself free:

"Who am I?"

While in bewilderment, a voice will bring
back your soul.
You should listen to it as it will walk you
through memories old.

It will make you realize the path you have
covered so far,
And help you rejoice in all the decisions you
took alone in the dark.

Wherever the world might take you,
Always remember that I will be proud of you.

A Small Girl

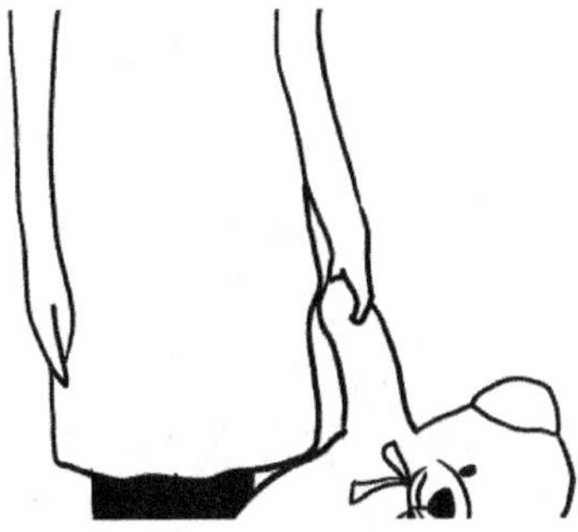

At six, I wandered the mall with my parents
carefree,
Then the manager smiled and said, "Let her
stay with me."
And my parents, so trusting, left me behind,
I realised his hands turned cruel, no safe
touch to find.
I was a girl so small, harmed by a world
unkind.

At seven, in school, I ate without care,
Then older boys dragged me, unaware.
They stole my food and bullied me still,
Said, "Tell no one, or it'll be worse, you'll feel."

I was a girl so small who was silenced, under
their cruel will.

At ten, on a trip, with joy in the air,
From the temple we left, with no signs of
despair.
But then a cop's stare pierced through my
soul,
His gaze made me shiver, a feeling so cold.
I was a girl so small, trapped in a fear's toll.

At fourteen, in school, as I walked the hall,
Two shadows loomed, making me feel so
small.
Their vile touch, with smiles of disgrace,
Left disgust and fear etched on my face.
I was a girl so small, lost to the world's cruel
call.

At eighteen, on a crowded bus so tight,
Two men sat beside me, stealing my light.
Their hands crept close, my heart felt fear,
I left the bus, wiping a silent tear.
I was a girl so small, hurt in a world unclear.

My stories are endless, my pain runs deep,
At every stage, fear haunts my sleep.
Love couldn't stay, for touch breaks me down,
I need time to heal, yet I feel I might drown.
I am a girl so small, lost in the world I've
known.

Imperfection In Depths:

Worked hard to get a body fit,
keeping in mind that the society has a
convention sweet
Dressed well, just how everyone likes,
But still walking with discomfort from those
dark dives

Walking with confidence gained through so
much struggles
Why do I lose it for a word bad?
The mirror smiles at me everyday as the dawn
unfold,
Yet, the nightfall finds me scared and cold.

Today, let me be my mirror and remind me...

Girl, you are perfect in your highs and lows,

Your beauty shines and it always shows.
Don't let others words, so harsh, so small,
Define your worth because you're above it all.

They'll point at flaws to mask their own,
Afraid to stand, they cast the stone.
Even if perfect by their written design,
They'll dig for flaws in what's divine.

Your scars, your skin, your weight, your
height,
Are gifts that make you your own light.
Do you mask these marks with shades that
shine,
Afraid the world won't see you fine?

Today, I'll tell you something clear,
Wear makeup only if it brings YOU cheer.
It's your joy that the make-up should define,
Not the thought that your beauty's not fine.

Who claimed that beauty must conform,
To flawless skin or a perfect form?
Did a story define what's right or wrong,
Or do movies sing this hollow song?

Is it the screens that shape our view,
With flawless forms and a narrow hue?
But beauty, my love, is undefined,
It's in every heart, in every mind.

Beauty is boundless and free,
A truth that lives in you and me.
No height or weight can cage your glow,
It's the soul within that makes you so.

See yourself for all that you hold,
A vibrant story that is rich, and bold.
The world may judge, but it's their loss,
Their standards are flawed and their lines
crisscrossed.

Let go of what the world may say,
Their view of beauty fades anyway.
Cherish your worth, your growth and your
fire,
For that's the beauty to inspire.

Hard To Love

While my fingers draw on the misty glass,
I sit and wonder, as the moments pass.
Is it the way I am, or the other things I do,
That people find it so hard to love me too?

Everyone's comfort is not the same;
Each heart seeks love, its own quiet flame.
But now I question myself with a silent plea,
Is my version of love too hard to be?

When arguments arise, I choose to let go,
Believing their struggles cut deeper than I know.
But can't they see— I hurt sometimes too?

All I need is love and a voice that says, "I am
with you."

I believed loving me was no heavy task,
I came with answers, you didn't need to ask.
Isn't it simple, to love someone who shows
Exactly the ways their heart truly glows?

If I hang up, don't let it end that way,
Call me back, show you care to stay.
If I'm shouting, it's my pain in disguise,
Hoping you'll see through my teary eyes.

I say a thousand times how much I care,
But you trust my words only when in despair.
I try so hard to be perfect for all,
Yet I wonder where I let it fall.

My Wish for Invisible Things

In this cumbersome world, why can't I live
like a free bird?
Why must I always ask, *"Why?"*
Why do I always carry the weight of society's
gaze?
I wish I could vanish,
Invisible to the world,
So I could be free—
Free to live, free to be.
To dance, unrestrained.
To sing,
With the heart unburdened, unafraid,
No judgments cast, no pointing fingers—
Just the rhythm of my soul,

Unseen, unbroken.
But simply vanishing isn't enough.
I wish for wings,
Wings to soar beyond the limits,
To fly high in the boundless sky—
A sky of true freedom,
Where no walls divide,
Where no one is less,
But all are equal, all are light.
I wish,
Oh how I wish,
To live—to truly live—
My own life,
Untouched by the world's demands,
Untethered from the chains that bind me,
Untethered from the chains that bind me,
Free to be *me*.

www.ingramcontent.com/pod-product-compliance
Lightning Source LLC
Chambersburg PA
CBHW061258140726

47998CB00006B/2267